LUFTWAFFE AT WAR

German Elite Pathfinders

Sometimes no special cranes were available to lift aircraft and the 'black men' (the ground crew, whose nickname came from their all-black attire) had to do it by muscle power alone as seen here. They are lifting the rear fuselage of one of their He 111s. In the background, to the left, is a Ju 52 used to transport spare parts and equipment to keep the unit operational.

LUFTWAFFE AT WAR

German Elite Pathfinders

KG 100 in Action

Manfred Griehl

Greenhill Books
LONDON

Stackpole Books
PENNSYLVANIA

Greenhill Books

German Elite Pathfinders: KG 100 in action first published 2000 by Greenhill Books, Lionel Leventhal Limited, Park House, 1 Russell Gardens, London NW11 9NN
www.greenhillbooks.com
and
Stackpole Books, 5067 Ritter Road, Mechanicsburg, PA 17055, USA

British Library Cataloguing in Publication Data
Griehl, Manfred
German elite pathfinders: KG 100 in action. – (Luftwaffe at war)
1.Germany. Luftwaffe. Kampfgruppe 100 – History
2.World War, 1939–1945 – Aerial operations, German
3.World War, 1939–1945 – Regimental histories – Germany
I. Title
940.5'44943

ISBN   1-85367-424-9

Library of Congress Cataloging-in-Publication Data available

Designed by DAG Publications Ltd
Design by David Gibbons
Layout by Anthony A. Evans

Printed in Singapore

LUFTWAFFE AT WAR
GERMAN ELITE PATHFINDERS
KG 100 IN ACTION

Early in 1934 the Secretary of Aviation, Erhard Milch, ordered Dr Plendl to begin the development of a secret navigation system called X-*Verfahren* (the 'X-system'). As a radio-beam navigation aid, this would allow German bomber crews to locate distant targets by day or night, irrespective of the weather. The research work was carried out by a department of the *Deutsche Versuchsanstalt für Luftfahrt* or DVL (the German Aviation Experimental Institute), which worked with the *Erprobungsstelle der Luftwaffe* (*Luftwaffe* Test Establishment) based at Rechlin on Lake Müritz. By December 1935 it was possible to navigate over distances of some 550 km flying at an altitude of 6000 m. First trials were carried out with a Ju 52/3m (D-ADEH) whose crew succeeded in bombing an area of 90,000 m² in central Germany. From 1 May 1935 all experimental work on the X-beam system was taken over by the *E-Stelle* at Rechlin. An experimental unit was established, comprising Ju 52/3m aircraft fitted with the new system. From 1935 to 1940 some thirty X-*Sendestationen* (X-beam transmitting stations) were installed all over Germany to allow further operations over eastern and western Europe.

By 1 November 1937 the *Luftnachrichtenschule und Versuchsregiment* (Air Signals Training and Experimental Regiment) was established at Köthen but was not part of the *Heeres Nachrichtenschule* (Army Signals School). All units belonging to the regiment, commanded by *Oberstleutnant* Heinrich Aschenbrenner, became operational by early December. On 1 January 1938 the experimental unit of the regiment, 7/*LnSchule und Versuchsregiment*, led by *Oberleutnant* Hermann Schmidt, was equipped with twelve Ju 52s. The crews carried out several long-range missions to the Canary Islands and to Tripoli in North Africa.

During summer 1938 the *Luftwaffe* established a *Flugfunkerschule und Versuchskommando* (Radio Operators' Training and Experimental Command), renamed the *Luftnachrichtenabteilung* 100, or *LnAbt* 100, (Air Signals Detachment 100) on 26 August that year. In the autumn it received its first Do 17U *Führungsmaschinen* (literally 'leader-machines', or 'pathfinders') but due to its narrow fuselage it was impossible to install the X-beam system in the Dornier. After a training phase the *LnAbt* 100 took part in the Poland campaign. The first operational mission was carried out on the night of 3/4 September to a target near the small town of Palmiry. On 18 November 1939, following the occupation of Poland the unit was renamed *Kampfgruppe* 100 (KGr 100) '*Wiking*'. As an independent unit, '*Wiking*' was known solely by the abbreviation 'KGr' 100, whereas most *Kampfgruppen* names simply took the form of Roman numeral prefixes which preceded the parent *Kampfgeschwader* (KG) number. KGr 100 was not initially a subdivision of any of the existing *Geschwader*, though it was later to form part of a new parent unit (*see below*). After its formation, KGr 100 left the *Luftnachrichtentruppe* (Air Signals Branch) and became a real combat unit. An unarmed X-beam mission, ordered by the Führer, was carried out on 20 December 1939 under the command of *Oberleutnant* Schmidt whose crew was sent to the British capital to check the security of the X-beam system over large distances. Early in January 1940 only one Do 17 and one He 111 belonged to the *Stab* (staff) of KGr 100. Both of KGr 100's *Staffeln* were equipped with He 111Hs. Of twenty-four bombers only thirteen were ready for action over Western Europe in early 1940.

The unit operated against enemy vessels on the North Sea between January 1940 and the early summer, and took part in the Norwegian campaign of that year. Under the command of *Luftflottenkommando* 5 (led by *Generaloberst* Milch) KGr 100 was sent out to destroy Norwegian anti-aircraft positions and coastal batteries. The unit was also used for anti-submarine and anti-shipping missions near the Norwegian coast.

During summer 1940 the first new He 111H-3 fitted with X-beam equipment (*X-Gerät*) arrived at Lüneburg. From there the *Gruppe* was transferred to Vannes in Brittany where more than five X-beam radio stations had been installed in order to intensify the air war over Britain. The first pathfinder missions over Britain took place during August 1940. Twenty aircraft of *Kampfgruppe* 100 targeted the Nuffield factory in Birmingham with the help of the X-beam. The unit was subsequently used to lead bombing raids on targets all over the British Isles. Long-range missions to Liverpool and Glasgow were carried out between December 1940 and April 1941. Crews of KGr 100 took part in the last heavy attack on London on the night of 11/12 May 1941. Some crews belonging to the *Kampfgruppe* were engaged in raids on shipping targets and on ports along the southern coast Britain. Armed reconnaissance missions were carried out in June and July 1941.

After the German attempt to besiege the British Isles with the *Luftwaffe* and minor forces of the *Kriegsmarine* failed, *Kampfgruppe* 100 was transferred to Terespol behind the Eastern Front where the unit was used to assist the *Luftwaffe* to attack the Russian capital. Together with KG 28 and parts of KG 4 and KG 26, KGr 100 successfully bombed industrial targets in the Moscow area. In 1942 KGr 100 operated over the southern part of the Eastern Front where it was engaged in several costly missions up to 1943.

On 29 November 1941, *Kampfgeschwader* 100 (KG 100) '*Wiking*' was established from KGr 100 and other units. It took the form of a well-equipped He 111 unit divided into a *Geschwaderstab* with four flying *Kampfgruppen*. One of the *Gruppen* under the command of the newly created KG 100 was the former *Ergänzungsstaffel* (replacement squadron) of KGr 100. It was desig-

nated as IV/KG 100 '*Wiking*' and retained its original role of *Ergänzungsstaffel* until 20 August 1944.

On 15 December 1941 the old KGr 100 became I *Kampfgruppe* of KG 100 '*Wiking*'. The unit had by now flown pathfinder missions during the Battle of Britain and had operated over the Russian Front using the Y-navigation system. Because most attack units of the *Luftwaffe* were used against Russian targets, only a few *Staffeln* could be sent to continue the air raids against British towns, harbours and industrial targets. Among them was 2 *Staffel* of KG 100. It was the nucleus for the operational testing of new tactical navigation methods over the British Isles from March 1942. The unit was called *Eprobungs– und Lehrkommando* 100 (Trials and Evaluation Command 100), later renamed *Erprobungs– und Lehrkommando* XY.

On 12 January 1942 I *Gruppe* landed at Focsani in Romania followed by its ground echelon two days later. A few days later the crews carried out attacks on heavy cruisers in the Straits of Kerch, the Black Sea and the harbour at Sevastopol. Although many hits on Russian vessels were reported by the *Luftwaffe*, the enemy's anti-aircraft units were responsible for the loss of several He 111Hs. Besides bombing attacks made on ships, the crews of I/KG 100 tried to sink enemy vessels with air-dropped mines in the shipping routes along the Black Sea coast. Because there were not enough German fighters available to protect their bomber forces, the KG 100 lost many men to fighters of the Red Air Force.

The former 4 *Staffel* of KG 26 was incorporated into I/KG 100 on 31 May 1942 in order to increase the number of missions flown over Russia. Between July 1942 and February 1943 I/KG 100 attacked targets over large distances. Besides Sukhumi and Grozny in the Caucasus, shipping targets near the mouth of the Volga were bombed during several raids. In summer 1942 I/KG 100 hit targets in the Stalingrad area. Railway lines and stations had become important targets and were bombed to prevent the enemy bringing up reinforcements and equipment.

The complete I/KG 100 was renamed I *Gruppe* of *Kampfgeschwader* 4 on 10 October 1943, though it simultaneously served under the command of KG 100 '*Wiking*'. This *Gruppe* then became III *Gruppe* of *Kampfgeschwader* 1

'Hindenburg' on 31 May 1944. Throughout much of this time the *Gruppe* was engaged in costly missions under the command of *Luftflottenkommando* 4 (led by *Generaloberst* von Richthofen). The Soviets threatened the German forces in the Caucasus and moved steadily towards the Crimea. After the German 6th Army was besieged by the Red Army at Stalingrad, the He 111 crews of I/KG 100 were ordered to assist the encircled German divisions by delivering ammunition, food and equipment by airdrop to enable the encircled troops to continue fighting. The Soviet encirclement was not broken and Stalingrad was lost. After the loss of the city and the 6th Army, I/KG 100 was withdrawn from operational service and re-equipped with He 111H-11s and H-16s. On 18 April 1943 the *Gruppe* mounted a series of air raids after being transferred to Stalino airfield. Mines were airdropped over the Volga. Early in May 1943 the 'Molotov' tank factories were hit by a composite group of the *Staffeln* of I/KG 100. In July the unit was needed for Operation 'Zitadelle', the last great German offensive in the east, launched in July 1943. But the German forces were on the retreat, moving steadily westward.

The II *Gruppe* of KG 100, which formerly served as III/KG 26, joined KG 100 on 15 December 1941. The II *Gruppe* operated from airfields positioned behind the central sector of the Eastern Front. Early in February 1942 II/KG 100 was sent to northern France. Their He 111Hs were handed over to I/KG 28. New He 111H-6s were delivered to II/KG 100 at Poix but before the handover could be completed the unit was engaged in an air raid on Hull, losing two of its existing He 111Hs. A few weeks later II/KG 100 flew to Kalamaki near Athens to operate in the Mediterranean. On 28 April 1942 fifteen He 111s of II/KG 100 together with twenty-five Ju 88s of *Lehrgeschwader* 1 carried out a night attack on targets in the region of Alexandria. Among the key targets were the harbour at Alexandria and the Suez Canal.

In June 1942 several Allied airfields in North Africa were bombed by He 111H-6s of II/KG 100. The following month saw further action over the Mediterranean Sea. At night the well-trained flyers of the 'Wiking' *Geschwader* tried to interdict the lines of communication of the British forces and destroy targets in the heart of the battle zone at El Alamein. Later in the year, II/KG 100 was sent to Catania on Sicily to prevent Allied forces invading the southern part of the Axis-controlled region. Desperate missions were carried out to support German ground forces in Tunisia. By the end of 1942, only four out of the seventeen remaining crews of II/KG 100 were completely operational. In April 1944 after many more missions the operational strength of the II *Gruppe* was lower than ever. The unit was withdrawn from active operations and sent to Graz on Usedom Island in the Baltic Sea.

One *Einsatzstaffel* (operational squadron) of KG 100, consisting of twelve crews with seventeen He 111H-6s, remained in Greece. This unit came under the command of *Luftflottenkommando* 2 (under *Generalfeldmarschall* Kesselring) and was needed to attack British forces all over the Greek islands. After one particular British raid on the Eleusis airfield the *Einsatzstaffel* lost its last aircraft and was disbanded on 10 November 1943.

The *Erprobungs– und Lehrkommando* 15 was raised on 20 April 1943 from parts of the II/KG 100 to test and introduce new air-to-ground weapons. At the end of April 1943 parts of II/KG 100 were used to form *Erprobungsstaffel* (test squadron) KG 100 which ended its career on 10 November 1944.

The remaining *Staffeln* of II *Gruppe* saw action until 31 May 1944. At that time 6/KG 100 was substituted with 8/KG 100. During the following month II/KG 100 operated all over Western Europe. The *Gruppe* was finally disbanded on 2 February 1945 because there was no opportunity to continue offensive operations due to lack of fuel and to the overwhelming air superiority of the Allies.

The III *Gruppe* of KG 100 'Wiking' was built up from units formerly belonging to *Aufklärungsgruppe (See)* 126 (Martime Reconnaissance Wing 126) on 20 September 1942. In October the *Gruppe* flew one Bv 138 (a three-engined flying boat) and eighteen Ar 196s (single-engined floatplanes) and some fifteen He 111s. It was planned to introduce thirty-six He 111H-14/trops ('tropicalised'). Parts of III/KG 100 operated over the Mediterranean Sea and carried out attacks in North Africa. The *Gruppe* was based at Salamis near Athens and was commanded by *Major* Schulz. In February 1943 it reverted to *Aufk-*

lärungsgruppe (See) 126 and left the *Geschwader*. On 20 April 1943 KGrzbV 21 (which had formerly flown transport missions to Stanlingrad) became the new III *Gruppe* of KG 100 and served in the 'Wiking' *Geschwader* until 7 September 1944 when *Oberkommandoluftwaffe* (OKL) ordered the *Gruppenstab* and all three *Staffeln* belonging to III/KG 100 to disband.

Later in 1943 the II and III *Gruppen* of KG 100 were re-established with new crews and an entirely new kind of naval weapon: guided glider bombs. Instead of He 111s both units were equipped with Do 217E-5s and K-2s in early summer 1943. Both types could be used to carry the glider bombs for anti-shipping raids. The *Gruppen* were transferred to southern France in readiness for operations. In July 1943 some smaller units operated from southern Italy. Early in September 1943, III/KG 100 carried out fourteen missions against the Italian navy which was preparing to surrender to the Western Allies. The Italian battleship *Roma* was sunk by two FX 1400 Fritz-X glider bombs. The crews were then concentrated at Istres to attack the Allied landings at Salerno. Allied convoys were also attacked but with only minor success. The end of 1943 saw glider bombs hit a few merchant ships before Allied forces landed at Anzio. Night by night III *Gruppe* was engaged in defensive missions but could not prevent the Allied forces enlarging their beachhead.

The II and III *Gruppen* of the 'Wiking' *Geschwader*, which were equipped with Do 217Es and Ks, were also trained to fly the heavy bomber He 177A in order to carry out attacks against enemy vessels in the Bay of Biscay and the Atlantic Ocean because the Heinkel had a longer operational range than the Dornier.

In late 1943 OKL decided to launch an operation against targets in the British Isles: Operation 'Steinbock' ('Ibex'), which became known as the 'baby blitz'. The operation was to be carried out with the bombers of KG 6, KG 30, KG 51, KG 54, KG 76 and KG 100, which were concentrated in northern Germany and parts of the occupied territories to the west. On 21 January 1944 the operational order arrived to attack industrial targets in London. With the He 177A-3s of 3/KG 100, a total of 227 bombers headed for their target. Due to the British air defences, which included night-fighters and anti-aircraft batteries, twenty-five German crews were shot down, while eighteen more failed to return due to technical difficulties. Three He 177s were shot down or severely damaged that day. The raids continued on the following nights. Again, on 4 February 1944, 240 German bombers launched attacks on British targets marked by pathfinders of I *Gruppe* of KG 66. The IX *Fliegerkorps* tried to operate as many bombers as possible to destroy all the designated targets. Due to many casualties and raids on the German airfields the number of available bombers was reduced. Only 125 of them carried out the last attack on London on the night of 25/26 April 1944. A few raids on Hull and Portsmouth followed.

Early in May 1945 the He 177s belonging to 2/KG 100 and 3/KG 100 were withdrawn from Rheine and Chateudun and flown to Fassberg. At the end of May 1944 I/KG 100 was re-established as I/KG 1 to see action over the Eastern Front. After severe losses the *Kampfgruppe* was disbanded.

A fourth *Gruppe* of *Geschwader* 'Wiking' was responsible for training new crews. IV/KG 100 which had been part of the *Geschwader* since November 1941, received a fourth *Staffel* (13/KG 100) on 20 April 1943. The unit was renamed *Erprobungs– und Lehrkommando* 36 on 31 July 1943. On 20 July 1944 another *Staffel* belonging to the 'Wiking' *Geschwader*, 12/KG 100, was re-established as 3 *Ergänzungs-Kampfgruppe* 177 (Replacement Bomber Wing 177). The IV *Gruppe* was disbanded on 20 August 1944 after there was no longer any need to train new crews for offensive raids with KG 100. The *Geschwaderstab* set up in late in 1941 was also disbanded on 20 August 1944. Thus, only two *Gruppen* of the 'Wiking' *Geschwader* – the II/KG 100 and III/KG 100 – were available for further operations. While the Allies landed on the shores of Normandy the remaining KG 100 crews suffered many more losses which finally caused the units to be declared ineffective and were disbanded.

Only the He 177s formerly used by II/KG 100 and based at Aalborg in Denmark remained operational until early 1945. Later the aircraft were scrapped after the engines had been dismantled. The operational life of KG 100 'Wiking' was over. Several members of the aircrews and ground crews were taken over by *Luftwaffe* paratroop units and saw the war's end fighting as infantry.

The H-1, H-3 and H-6 versions of the He 111 were among the most used bombers of KG 100 'Wiking'. By 1943 these variants were replaced by more powerful He 111H-11s, H-14s, H-16s and H-20s. The aircraft shown here is a H-6 series He 111 which could carry bomb loads of up to 1800 kg under the main fuselage.

This 2/KG 100 'Wiking' He 177A-3 (6N+HK) is pictured early in 1944 at Schwäbisch-Hall where these aircraft were prepared for operations with remote-controlled glider bombs. In front of the aircraft is a VW *Kübelwagen* (*Kübel* literally meaning 'pail' or 'container') taking one of the crews (commanded by *Oberleutnant* Kuntz) to their bomber.

One of the *Kampfgruppe* 100's He 111H-1s targets a merchant ship near the Norwegian coastline during the Norwegian campaign. Several bombing raids and reconnaissance missions were carried out over a few weeks. Together with crews of KG 26 'Löwen' (Lion) *Geschwader* KGr 100 was engaged in attacking British transport vessels trying to support Allied ground forces in Norway.

A lonesome He 111H patrolling the Norwegian coast in early 1940. Because only a few German bomber squadrons were available over northern Europe these aircraft were often forced to operate without fighter protection and without adequate ground crew support. Consequently only limited tactical success was achieved by the end of the hostilities. Norwegian fighters succeeded in shooting down and damaging a significant number of German combat aircraft.

A formation of He 177s of 1 *Staffel*, I *Gruppe*, KG 100 '*Wiking*' on their way to new positions in southern France early in 1944. The aircraft show the standard camouflage used for many aircraft employed on anti-shipping missions.

Three graphic shots of a burning He 177A-3 hit during the raid on 25 April 1944 at Schwäbisch-Hall in Southern Germany. Although the *Fliegerhorst* (*Luftwaffe* airfield) fire service together with the ground crew of IV/KG 100 did their best, four of the huge combat aircraft were heavily damaged by bombs. After receiving damage to the fuel tanks, two other nearby aircraft exploded. Altogether six He 177s were completely destroyed.

Another view of the devastation wreaked by Allied bombers at Schwäbisch-Hall. One of the He 177A-3s of IV/KG 100 has burst into flames after being hit. In the centre, an aircraft taxis along the concrete runway as it tries to escape.

Above: One of the first He 111Ps and Hs to equip the *Luftnachrichtenabteilung* 100 (Air Signals Detachment 100) at Köthen in summer 1938. Up until then it had operated a few Ju 52s and Do 17Us. The He 111s were fitted with an improved X-beam navigational system. To check the new wireless sets the crews undertook long-range flights to Africa and over the sea.

Below: Oversized *Balkenkreuze* were used for a short period on German warplanes, as shown here on this He 111 belonging to 1/*Kampfgruppe* 100. These were intended to minimise the risk of being shot down by one of their own AA-batteries. Additional antennae can be seen on the spine of this He 111. The upper machine-gun has been removed to prevent the gunner from shooting off the aircraft's aerial masts. This modification was made during pre-war trials.

Opposite page, top: The tactical markings on these He 111s, which were fitted with the X-Gerät, showed that they belonged to KGr 100. The '6N' to the left of the cross was the *Gruppe* code (it was also retained as the *Geschwader* code for KG 100), while the 'I' to the right of the cross is the individual aircraft code ('I' signifying that this bomber is the ninth aircraft in its particular *Staffel*). The last letter, K, is the code for 2 *Staffel* of KGr 100. All of the aircraft are painted in standard splinter camouflage. The *Balkenkreuze* were later reduced in size.

Opposite page, bottom: Early in 1940 *Kapitän zur See* Helmut Grubbe, who served with KGr 100, suggested a black

Viking ship with white shields and a white-and-red sail, during a competition held to find an appropriate emblem. His proposal was chosen and later taken over by *Kampfgeschwader* 100 which also subsequently received the name '*Wiking*' (Viking).

Above: Two bomber aircrewmen during last preparations for a night mission over Britain. Both wear the standard summer-weight flying clothing, an overall called *Schutzanzug für Sommer* KSo/34. They wear the field service cap whose unofficial name was *Schiffchen* (little ship) on account of its shape.

Above: Inside the glazed cockpit of an He 111H bomber heading for its target somewhere in the southern part of Great Britain. Because no enemy fighters have been sighted the forward gun position is not yet being manned by one of the crew. The navigation instruments are on the left side of the panel across the top of the picture, while the engine control instruments are on the right.

Below: Over Norway KGr 100 showed great skill when carrying out long-range raids on well-defended targets. This He 111H bomber is crossing the fjords where emergency landings were notoriously dangerous.

Above: This Heinkel is ready for the next mission over Norway in 1940. Besides Andalsnes, Bodö and Narvik, enemy installations such as the forts near Dröbak and coastal shipping were the most important targets. During the first phase of the campaign KGr 100 was forced to use frozen lakes as landing grounds because so few airfields had been captured.

Below: Two lonely He 111Hs crossing a mountain chain in Norway. Both aircraft belong to 1 *Staffel* of KGr 100 and have been sent to attack a Norwegian stronghold at the end of April 1940. Despite the snowy landscape the upper surfaces of the bombers remain in standard dark-green camouflage.

One of KGr 100's He 111s being refuelled by the ground crew on the frozen surface of the Norwegian Lake Jonsvannet. The fuel has been transported by Ju 52s of the *Kampfgruppen* zbV (temporary transport units) whose purpose was to carry out airborne drops when the supply aircraft were unable to land.

Above: An airman belonging to KGr 100 which was commanded by *Hauptmann* von Casimir during the Norwegian campaign. His command post was at Trondheim after the town had been occupied by German forces. The He 111H-3 shown here, the ninth bomber (as indicated by the white 'I' on the wing leading-edge, right) of 1 *Staffel* of the *Kampfgruppe*, is only armed with MG 15s. Similarly armed He 111s suffered some losses inflicted by British and Norwegian fighters.

Below: This picture was taken by the *Beobachter* (observer) during one of the long-range missions over Norway. He was responsible for the close defence of the aircraft with an MG 15 machine-gun. Because the range of German fighters was too short to give the bombers protection all the way to the target, Allied fighters shot down four He 111s of KGr 100. The last of these was on 29 May 1940: *Hauptmann* Artur von Casimir's aircraft. He became a POW.

Left: From Norway the aircraft were sent to German-occupied airfields at Dinord, Caen, Vannes and Chartres in France during summer 1940. From these airfields KGr 100's crews carried out a bombing mission over Great Britain. The first target bombed by the He 111H shown here was near Birmingham. During that raid, on 13 August 1940, one He 111H-3 (6N+BH) was attacked by RAF fighters. The wireless operator, *Unteroffizier* Fritz Dorner, baled out of the aircraft which returned to France, despite being damaged.

Above: An He 111H-1 is loaded with small bombs used as target indicators. By marking out targets on the ground, various kinds of bombs of this sort were introduced to show the following aircraft where to drop their loads. The first He 111s used by KGr 100 and other combat units of the *Luftwaffe* were only equipped to carry up to eight 250 kg bombs – a total weight of 2000 kg.

Left: This He 111H-3 (6N+EK) belongs to 2/KGr 100. Together with He 111H-1s this aircraft operated over Britain at the end of August 1940. Eight crews of 1/KGr 100 and 2/KGr 100 and airmen from KG 27, KG 40, KG 51 and KG 55 were sent out to destroy targets in the Liverpool area. During these raids the battleship HMS *Prince of Wales* was hit by bombs dropped by a KGr 100 crew.

Above: These bombers have been fuelled and filled with bombs by the ground crews for a forthcoming operation over the British Isles. The forward MG 15 machine-guns were later replaced with 20 mm MG FFs for bombardments on small ships along the British coast. The H-3 version differed from the H-1 in having port and starboard waist MG 15s installed.

Below: When more powerful versions of the He 111H became operational with the *Luftwaffe* it was possible to carry loads of 1000 kg beneath the central part of the fuselage. To move these heavy loads on the ground they were put on sleds, as shown here, and towed by a lorry or a small captured tank. Those shown here are SC 1000s painted all-over grey. They are fitted with the new circular tail units instead of the earlier unit of four braced tail fins.

Right: This crew waits in front of their bomber on a French airfield in the last minutes before embarking on the next mission. Note the kapok life jacket at their feet.

Above: A close-up view of the tail fin of an He 111H (serial number 5105) which is being cleaned by a member of the ground crew who is working without his uniform jacket due to the hot summer, somewhere in northern France in 1940. The white vertical bar above the swastika is probably the aircraft's identification code, unusually applied to the tail.

Top left: *Feldwebel* Horst Götz is standing on the right with the rest of his crew in front of 5105. Most of them are wearing Walter P 38 pistols for self-defense in the event of being shot down over enemy territory. They wear the standard *Luftwaffe* field uniform and flight cap.

Bottom left: Several aircraft of KGr 100 were damaged in action over the British Isles and returned to their French bases in bad condition with wounded crew members and only a few litres of fuel in the damaged wing tanks. Here a recovery crew readies the fuselage of one of the damaged aircraft for transportation to a repair unit.

Below: The engines of He 111H-3 6N+EK, an aircraft equipped with the X-beam system, are tested before take off. The *X-Gerät* antennae can be seen on the top of the fuselage. This aircraft is painted in the standard camouflage while the *Balkenkreuze* are larger than on other aircraft.

Right: The crew of this He 111H of 1 *Staffel* of KG 100's I *Gruppe* hold the tailwheel of their aircraft which failed on landing after returning from a raid on Britain. This pathfinder has three antennae on the fuselage. It had been operated by another, unidentified, *Staffel* as indicated by the overpainted markings.

Opposite page, bottom: When no refuelling lorries were available, members of the ground crew were forced to refuel the large bombers by hand. Erich Schwippe and his assistant carry out this difficult job of filling all the tanks of the He 111.

Above: An *Unteroffizier* of 2/KG 100 has just left the entrance hatch of his He 111. He carries the film cassette in one hand and the large remote-controlled camera in the other. He is taking them to the unit's specialists so that the pictures taken during the last mission can be developed and the *Reihenbildanlage* (automatic camera) can be checked.

Opposite page, top: Hans Götz's crew, all of whom have been decorated with the *Eisernes Kreuz I Klasse* (Iron Cross, First Class), is visited by an officer of the *Kriegsmarine*. Traces of damage to Horst Götz's He 111H-3 are discernible. It had flown many missions over Britain. All-white markings and insignia on the camouflage were overpainted with black shortly after the start of night raids.

Right: In order to calibrate its compass, this He 111H-3 stands on a so-called *Kompensierungsstand* (compass stand). This pathfinder, 6N+EK, is fully armed and equipped to ensure correct calibration.

Left: A group of He 111H-3s and H-4s of KGr 100 heading for targets in Britain. To protect themselves the crews fly in close combat boxes to intensify their defensive fire in the event of attack by enemy fighters. This group has the firepower of thirty-six MG 15s but the lack of heavier weapons was a drawback.

Opposite page, bottom: After being damaged by mines the *Wolf*, a German torpedo boat (a small destroyer), sank north of Dunkirk on 8 August 1941 with the loss of thirteen men. Here, a He 111 from KGr 100 coordinates the operations of the *Seenotstaffeln* (air-sea-rescue squadrons) and the *Kriegsmarine* to rescue the remaining crew.

Below: This formation belongs to 2 *Staffel* of KGr 100. To avoid being detected by British radar the aircraft fly at low-level over the North Sea. This had the added advantage of making it harder for enemy fighters to attack them.

Above: To avoid being spotted by enemy night-fighters most He 111H-3s and H-4s belonging to KGr 100 were painted all-over black like the aircraft shown here. The *Balkenkreuze* were overpainted except those on the upper wing surfaces. This aircraft has red spinners, indicating that it belongs to 2 *Staffel* of KGr 100.

Left: A close-up view of a He 111H-3 of 1/KGr 100 standing near the runway on an airfield in northern France. The original paint shows through on the spinner and the bombsight cover where the black camouflage, a temporary distemper, has worn away. The white spinners indicate the aircraft belongs to 1 *Staffel* of KGr 100. The bomb-bay doors are open ready for bombs to be loaded.

Above: An *Unteroffizier* early in 1941 checks the Jumo 211Ds of a well-camouflaged He 111H-3 of KGr 100. The exhaust gases have burned away the black camouflage along the nacelle to show the bare metal underneath. The undercarriage legs are painted light grey.

Left: *Feldwebel* Horst Götz (third from left) and a few other NCOs together with members of the ground crew responsible for looking after this black-painted He 111H-3 posing in early summer 1941. Note the landing light and pitot tube on the wing leading-edge. The antennae on the fuselage show that this aircraft is equipped with the X-beam navigation system.

Opposite page, bottom: This unidentified He 111H-3 crew serving in KGr 100 are all NCOs. The bombsight can be seen just to the left of the *Feldwebel* on the far left. The yellow triangle next to the *Gruppen* emblem indicates that the aircraft uses 87-octane fuel. The 25 painted in white comprises the last two digits of the serial number.

Below: One of KGr 100's aircrew, possibly Heinz Bitter, is visited in northern France by a friend serving with another *Luftwaffe* unit. The man on the left is standing inside the aircraft and looking out over the opened roof hatch.

Right: *Feldwebel* Horst Götz (second left) and two *Unteroffiziere* pose before an He 111H of KGr 100 while the ground crew check the systems and the defensive armament of the heavy bomber. Inside the cockpit a *Luftwaffe Gefreiter* (aircraftman, first class) is working on the bombsight.

Below: An aerial view captured during the final phase of the bombing of the British Isles. Targets were widespread, though the capital bore the brunt of some of the heaviest attacks. On 11 May 1941 some 500 bombers took part in an attack on London. Of these aircraft 291 belonged to *Luftflotte* 3. Eleven He 111Hs of KGr 100 were used as pathfinders for the main attack.

Opposite page, bottom: This He 111H has been shot down. The pilot was forced to make an emergency landing in the sea. Because the surface of the sea was smooth the crew were able to enter their life raft without difficulty. The *Luftwaffe* concentrated a number of air-sea-rescue units along the occupied coast of the English Channel so that many British and German airmen were rescued.

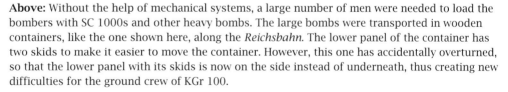

Above: Without the help of mechanical systems, a large number of men were needed to load the bombers with SC 1000s and other heavy bombs. The large bombs were transported in wooden containers, like the one shown here, along the *Reichsbahn*. The lower panel of the container has two skids to make it easier to move the container. However, this one has accidentally overturned, so that the lower panel with its skids is now on the side instead of underneath, thus creating new difficulties for the ground crew of KGr 100.

Opposite page, top: After sustaining damage to the tailwheel, this He 111H-3 of 1/KGr 100 awaits repair by the ground crew. After returning from a mission over Britain the pilot made a rough landing which caused the damage. The aircraft is equipped with the X-*Gerät*, has faded upper surfaces and may have been engaged in action several times over Western Europe between 1940 and 1941.

Left: This unusual view shows all three main antennae fixed on the top of the fuselage of an He 111H fitted with the X-beam navigation system. The dorsal position is fitted with a (7.9 mm) MG 15 machine-gun. During the night raids the defensive armament was often reduced to nose and dorsal positions because RAF nightfighters usually tried to shoot down the bombers from behind.

Opposite page, top: A group of Italian Air Force personnel with members of KGr 100 on an airfield on the Eastern Front.

Above: This He 111, 6N+MP, belongs to III *Gruppe* of KG 100 and is fitted with a Y-navigation system. The Y-antenna can be seen immediately behind the glazed cabin. The aircraft is being cleaned by the ground crew. The yellow stripe around the rear fuselage indicates that it is operating on the Eastern Front.

Below: After OKL ordered the intensification of attacks on Moscow on 19 July 1941, KGr 100 was sent to Terespol near Brest-Litovsk while the *Flugbetriebskompanie* (Airfield Service Company) together with a replacement unit, 10 *Ergänzungsstaffel*/KGr 100, and the *Luftnachrichten-kompanie* (Air Signals Company) remained in France. On the day of the attacks, the complete KGr 100 could only muster thirteen He 111H-3s, of which only three were serviceable.

Above: After their 500th mission this unidentified crew from KGr 100 is being congratulated by the commanding officer. From left to right: a *Gefreiter*, an *Unteroffizier*, a *Hauptmann*, an *Oberfeldwebel* and a *Feldwebel* wearing summer flying suits. They all seem relaxed after having survived one more mission.

Opposite page, top: When the units belonging to I/KG 100 attacked enemy positions on the battlefield, towns near the front line were also often hit, causing much destruction, as this picture shows.

Opposite page, bottom: A Russian town after a raid. Wooden housing typical of Russian towns burned easily and the fires quickly spread, often completely destroying the inner section of a town.

Opposite page: Horst Götz standing in front of his new He 111H-6 bomber which has just been transferred from Germany. The new aircraft allowed KG 100 to carry larger, far more destructive bombs on the external racks compared to the relatively small load that could be carried internally in the bomb-bay of the H-6's forerunners. Besides two SC 1000s it was possible to carry one large SC 1700 or SC 1800 or the SC 2500 'Max', the largest bomb used by the *Luftwaffe* in action over Russia.

Above: One of the He 111H-20s belonging to 4/KG 100 taxiing on its muddy airfield somewhere in Russia. The *Geschwader* code 6N – to the left of the fuselage cross – is about one-fifth its previous size, presumably to make identification by the enemy more difficult. The He 111H-20 was built for a variety of roles, including bomber, glider tug and transport plane. Note the electrically operated dorsal turret which houses a single 13 mm MG 131.

Below: One of II/KG 100's airfields near the front line illustrating the muddy conditions caused by rain and the lack of concrete runways. The mud hindered movement on the ground and increased the number of undercarriage failures. In the foreground is an SD 1000 armour-piercing bomb, while in the background there are several *Abwurfbehälter* AB 250 bomblet dispensers filled by small SD 2 (2 kg) and SD 5 (5 kg) bomblets which were scattered over a wide area when the dispensers opened in mid air.

Left: An aerial view of a devastated Kiev following a German bomber raid. It was only because of the limited number of German bombers available for operations on the Eastern Front that greater damage was avoided.

Below: A different kind of steel helmet from the standard German issue is being worn by this NCO belonging to KG 100 while operating in Greece. The captured British helmet he wears is a souvenir to show his family in Germany. The He 111H behind him belongs to III *Gruppe* of the '*Wiking*' *Geschwader*, engaged in fighting the British Navy in the Aegean Sea. The *Geschwader*'s aircraft also performed escort duties and were used on anti-shipping missions over the eastern Mediterranean.

Top right: This merchant ship has a lucky escape as three bombs dropped by an He 111H-6 and a H-11 of III/KG 100 land in the sea. Only a few vessels were sunk by KG 100 which mostly operated from the airfield at Kalamaki near Athens.

Right: Between late summer 1942 and February 1943 III *Gruppe* of KG 100 '*Wiking*' operated from different bases around Greece. After the *Aufklärungsgruppe (See)* 126 became part of the unit their Ar 196 floatplanes were given to other units. The III/KG 100 was then quickly re-equipped with new He 111H-6, H-11 and H-14 aircraft. One of the main duties of the unit was anti-submarine warfare.

52

Right: This aircraft, 6N+FH, was operated by 1/KG 100 until it crashed in North Africa after being intercepted by RAF fighters. The crew became POWs of the British.

Right: The He 111H-11 could carry all kinds of bombs, supply containers or torpedoes on its external racks. Most of the H-11s lost by KG 100 crashed over the Mediterranean and Southern Russia in 1942 and 1943. Because the Allied fighters had grown considerably in number the German Heinkel bombers could not fulfill their role without heavy losses.

Left: This Do 217E-5 (serial number 5554) is one of the first *Sonderkampfflugzeuge* (special bombardment aircraft) to be operated with Hs 293A rocket-assisted glider bombs, one of which can be seen here. This aircraft was operated by 6/KG 100 until it failed to return from a mission at Salerno on 13 September 1943. It was probably shot down by Allied nightfighters while attempting to attack the ships near the landings.

Below, left and right: Side and front views of a Hs 293A glider bomb suspended under the wing of a Do 217E-5. This weapon was tested for the first time in late 1940 near Karlshagen (Usedom Island) in the Baltic. The remote-controlled weapon had a speed of about 580 km/h and a range of 16,000 m when released at an altitude of 8000 m. Note the rocket booster beneath the bomb.

Above: *Feldwebel* Grabert and his crew standing in front of their Do 217E-5. The notice on the entrance hatch reads 'Walk around the aircraft to avoid contact with the propellers'. Normally the aircraft were flown with one Hs 293 and one huge fuel container under the opposite wing to allow the crew to carry out long-range missions over the sea. The aircraft is well-camouflaged for this kind of operation as it is painted in grey dapple.

Below: A Do 217E-5 (KG+YP) after a rough landing near the airport of Bergamo in Italy. The aircraft (serial number 5558) has sustained only minor damage after its belly landing on a flat meadow on 21 February 1944. Only the lower part of the fuselage, the propellers and parts of the nacelles have been damaged. The crew survived.

Right: A close-up view of the nose section of a Do 217K-2 *Sonderkampfflugzeug.* The K-2 differed from the normal bomber version, the K-1, having enlarged wings and the ability to carry one or two Fritz-X remote-controlled glider bombs under the inner wing sections. Additionally these aircraft had an improved wireless system, identified by the antennae along the wing leading-edges. The *Kutonase* (a horizontal metal strip which was looped around the nose just above the gun) was standard.

Right: A view into the glazed cockpit of a Do 217K. On the left sits the pilot in an armoured seat (*Einheitspanzersitz*) which was fitted to many different types of aircraft. Beside him sits the *Beobachter* (observer), responsible for guiding the glider bombs to their targets. In the upper centre of the picture is a rear-warning system and to the left of it is a *Reflexvisier* (reflector bombsight) used for conventional bombing.

Above: Three Do 217K-2s at their airfield at Istres in southern France. The special bombers belong to III *Gruppe* of KG 100 and are equipped with an optical rear-view system on the cabin roof. The aircraft are painted in the standard two-tone splinter camouflage and have light blue undersurfaces.

Below: This photograph of a Do 217K-2 (serial number 4536) of III/KG 100 was taken in Toulouse in the middle of 1944. The aircraft is ready to be loaded with two Fritz-X glider bombs. Aircraft like this were used to sink the Italian battleship *Roma* on 9 September 1943 with two heavy armour-piercing bombs. Instead of MG 15s the K-2 was fitted with MG 81s and MG 131s to improve its defensive capabilities.

Opposite: After one Fritz-X has hit the afterdeck of the *Roma* a second one can be seen heading towards the huge Littorio class battleship (which weighed 35,000 tons) coming in from the right (see centre right). *Unteroffizier* Eugen Degan directed the bomb by radio control from the front of the cockpit. During that mission the sister ship *Italia* was also hit by a Fritz-X but it managed to reach La Valetta on Malta. Two Italian destroyers were also damaged in the attack.

Above: An aerial view of two Do 217K-2s of III/KG 100 in action during one of the difficult day raids on Allied warships in late summer 1943. Between 11 and 17 September 1943 six of these missions were carried out escorted by German fighters. The targets were in the region of Salerno. Besides Do 217K-2s the less powerful E-5s were also used to try to stop the Allied landings but only one Allied cruiser and two destroyers were damaged.

Left: This Do 217K-2 crashed after being hit by Allied anti-aircraft fire over Salerno in September 1943. Due to the lack of spare parts it was impossible to repair the aircraft before Allied ground troops arrived. Under the right wing is a bomb pylon (ETC) for carrying a Hs 293 remote-controlled glider bomb. The *Balkenkreuz* design has been painted over part of the pylon.

Right, above and below: The officer here is *Major* (later *Oberstleutnant*) Bernhard Jope, commanding officer of KG 100 '*Wiking*'. He took command on 10 October 1943 from *Major* Fritz Auffhammer who had assumed command of KG 3. He is supervising the maintenance of this Do 217K bomber which is well camouflaged for anti-shipping missions. The NCO in charge of the ground crew carrying out the work, *Oberfeldwebel* Kuhn, reports on the progress of the work. The NCO on the right in each picture has brought a repaired wireless set to be installed in the rear of the glazed cockpit.

Opposite page, top: Despite the heat *Major* Jope wears the full service uniform of the *Luftwaffe* while checking the work of the ground crew. The two men to his right were nicknamed *Propellerputzer* ('propeller cleaners') and are engaged in changing one of the main wheels of the Do 217K-2 at Istres airfield.

Opposite page, bottom: At the well-equipped *Luftwaffe* airbase of Fassberg, near Hamburg, this He 177A-5 (serial number 550849) is ready for a test flight. The III/KG 100 received He 177A-3s at the end of 1943, and these aircraft were later replaced by more powerful variants early in 1944. Of the A-5s handed over to *Stab*/KG 100, 4/KG 100 and 6/KG 100, only six of them were lost.

Above: At Munich-Riem this He 177A-3 belonging to IV/KG 100 waits to take off to fly to Fassberg in September 1944. On the well-equipped airfield more He 177s wait with more than 120 other aircraft, some of them KG 100 Do 217K-1s, to have new wireless sets fitted before being transferred to other operational airbases.

Below: Two He 177A-1s standing at the airbase in Aalborg, Denmark, early in 1944. In the foreground is 6N+AN which belongs to 5/KG 100. At Aalborg the He 177s were dismantled and the DB 610 engines removed to be used in fighters of the *Reichsluftverteidigung* (Organisation for the Defence of the Reich). The long-range bombers were scrapped to provide materials for the construction of new fighter aircraft.

Above: Two aircraft of 8/KG 100 standing at Fassberg. Despite the fact that these aircraft belonged to the best equipped long-range combat aircraft operated by the *Luftwaffe* they were unable to make an impact on the war due to lack of aviation fuel. Some of the late He 177A-5s were rebuilt to carry wire-guided bombs after the Allies learned to intercept the signals used to guide the radio-controlled glider bombs.

Below: Because so little fuel was available it was possible to carry out only a limited number of training flights and all attempts to commence operations became impossible by

1944. Therefore the huge bombers were camouflaged, like the aircraft shown here, to prevent their being spotted and destroyed by Allied fighter-bombers.

Opposite page: This photograph of three members of an He 177A-5 crew led by *Hauptmann* Hans Schacke was taken at Aalborg in late summer 1944. From left to right: *Gefreiter* Adolf Dops (air gunner), *Obergefreiter* (leading aircraftman) Hans Balbach (air gunner) and *Unteroffizier* Hans Fontius (wireless operator). The aircraft (6N+DN) belongs to 5/KG 100. This picture shows the comparatively large dimensions of a DB 610A/B engine.

Opposite page top, and above: Two KG 100 victims of Allied low-level attacks. The new He 177A-5s of III *Gruppe* have been hit during conversion training. Due to the size of the He 177 it was an easy target on the ground. Only a few parts could be saved for spares.

Left: A photograph taken at Aalborg. *Hauptmann* Schacke's crew wait for one of the few training flights over Denmark and the Baltic Sea. All crew members wear the summer flight suit and life jackets. Only a few weeks later the men were given new occupations after their He 177s were scrapped. Most men serving with KG 100 were sent to *Luftwaffe* field units or paratroop units and had to learn to fight as infantry.

Above: Another shot of the He 177A-5 (6N+DN) commanded by *Hauptmann* Hans Schacke, also taken at Aalborg in summer 1944. In front of the aircraft stand the pilot, *Oberfeldwebel* Wilhelm Niederstadt, the observer, Schacke, and three fellow crew members. The A-5 is well camouflaged for operations over the sea.

Below: The He 177A-5 (serial number 550135) shown here at Aalborg belongs to II *Gruppe*. The photograph was taken at the time of the OKL order to dismantle all heavy bombers of II/KG 100. A few of the aircraft belonging to KG 100 continued to be operated for weather reconnaissance missions over the North Atlantic and the Arctic Ocean because the skilled crews could fulfil the demands of long-range missions in all weathers.

This photograph illustrates the limited space available to the tail gunner in an He 177. Many A-3s and A-5s were lost in France after the Allies advanced faster then estimated by the German Supreme Command. In summer 1944, the few remaining aircraft were destroyed by German personnel as they retreated to prevent the aircraft falling into enemy hands.

Opposite page, top: This crew succeeded in shooting down an American P-61 Black Widow nightfighter when returning from a mission over the Atlantic Ocean. This crew often carried one or two of their dogs on board their He 177 bomber. The aircraft is painted in two or more grey tones to render it less visible in murky conditions.

Opposite page, bottom: This view of the same crew and their dogs on a French airfield shows the relative size of the aircraft. Note the rear-view mirror on top of the cockpit to allow the pilot to see enemy fighters attacking from behind. This highly skilled crew was reported to have survived dangerous missions over the Mediterranean, the Bay of Biscay and the Atlantic Ocean.

Above: The tail section of a He 177A-3 (serial number 2618) housing an experimental twin 13 mm MG 131. A similar system was used in the tails of some Ju 188 variants. There is insufficient information to enable us to draw conclusions about whether this weapon arrangement was more effective than the more usual single 20 mm MG 151.

Below: One of the last He 177A-5s which crashed before being withdrawn from active service with KG 40 and KG 100. This aircraft was sent to Leipheim, south of Augsburg in Bavaria to be scrapped. Note the two-tone grey camouflage of the fuselage and the lower part of the nacelles. It seems that there is no *Balkenkreuz* on the upper wing surfaces. This photograph was taken in late 1944.

The tail of one of the last He 177s operated by I/KG 100 'Wiking' and which was engaged in the last attacks on British targets in 1944. After the failure of Operation 'Steinbock' – the 'baby blitz' of early 1944 – and the heavy losses of summer 1944, several He 177A-3s and A-5s were handed over to *Feldwerftabteilungen* (Field Workshop Detachments) and the aircraft were later captured by Allied ground troops in France. A very few of these aircraft were repaired and evaluated by the US Air Force and French Air Force at the end of World War II.